MUSTER POINTS

UNIVERSITY OF CALGARY
Press

MUSTER
POINTS

POEMS BY
LUCAS
CRAWFORD

Brave & Brilliant Series

ISSN 2371-7238 (Print) ISSN 2371-7246 (Online)

© 2023 Lucas Crawford

University of Calgary Press
2500 University Drive NW
Calgary, Alberta
Canada T2N 1N4
press.ucalgary.ca

LIBRARY AND ARCHIVES CANADA CATALOGUING IN PUBLICATION

Title: Muster points / poems by Lucas Crawford.
Names: Crawford, Lucas, author.
Series: Brave & brilliant series ; no. 32.
Description: Series statement: Brave & brilliant series ; no. 32 | Poems.
Identifiers: Canadiana (print) 20230224431 | Canadiana (ebook) 20230224458 | ISBN
    9781773854526 (hardcover) | ISBN 9781773854533 (softcover) | ISBN 9781773854557
    (EPUB) | ISBN 9781773854540 (PDF)
Classification: LCC PS8605.R43 M87 2023 | DDC C811/.6—dc23

The University of Calgary Press acknowledges the support of the Government of Alberta
through the Alberta Media Fund for our publications. We acknowledge the financial support
of the Government of Canada. We acknowledge the financial support of the Canada Council
for the Arts for our publishing program.

Printed and bound in Canada by Marquis
♻ This book is printed on Enviro Book Natural paper

Editing by Helen Hajnoczky
Cover art by Morgan Sea
Caricature on p. ii by Morgan Sea, 2022
Page design and typesetting by Melina Cusano

Forewarnings

Hello readers! Welcome to my book. Thanks for coming. I wanted to give you a personal word of caution and promise: this work contains many frank and explicit references to sex, gender, and the violences of various xenophobias (relating to race, queerness, size, and transgender). Of course it does! No muster point is utopian. (But speaking of utopian, can you imagine a world in which books that propagate gender norms or represent straight culture would require a content warning?) My wish for you and all of us is that poetry be allowed to surprise us, even upset us, remake our expectations, and send us off with unfamiliar ideas and feelings. If and when I've done that here, I'm lucky – as I am to have your time. Please enjoy responsibly.

FRONT HOLES

INCH BY INCH is how things enter me –
also how resources are extracted. Years after prom,
I asked a prairie seamstress to cut two feet off
my peacock gown for a drag queen number.
Please, she begged, *let's keep it longer – to here,
or even just to here?* With our incompatible systems,
giving an inch sacrifices at least a kilometre of the
Antigonish road on which you – jubilant, vomiting –
stumbled sideways to dim Boomer apartments.
Best to drag metaphors out of the imperial realm,
best to insist on the high snip and go.

An enduring crush thought she could fuck me
with a black baseball bat of a dildo, no ramp-up.
Having an audience didn't help.
These days I love to clean the house,
but it's not a perfect fit I'm after.
Before you fuck me, I can't know
if you'll fuck the last bit of girl out of me,
or fuck her back in. When you call a number
you can't be sure who will pick up. *Dial carefully*
is not an inspiring parable; besides, nobody carries
each other's numbers around these days.

In court, Subway insisted that the "foot-long" in
"foot-long sub" is symbolic, that eleven inches is
enough. In a different court, their spokesperson
defended having pursued little girls by arguing that,
having once been very fat, he did not know
how to court women. I too could find a patsy
in my past to account
for present ineptitude.   [. . . *Her?*]
But I could never separate wheat from chaff like others,
didn't want to. We flirt with her when I offer it all to you.
It's not that it's a road seldom taken. It's worn

well enough. Fantastical coaches have held me down
for impregnation. Imagined twenty-one year olds
with cottoned dogs have shown teen-me
how to feel good behind the park bathrooms.

There are words that work as front door passkeys.
Call it "call me a boy." Call it
       "ambivalent-identity-as-a-sex-toy."
       But you dizzy me in slow unnamable circles.
       O my meagre protections, bent
       in thin hands like dollar store trinkets.

I recently reminded another scholar-poet
not to end each poem with a conclusion.
Trust the reader. Let them
get there in their own way.

This, like other things, is about ceding control
and the illusion that you've ever had it.
Letting those who enter here see you
as they will see you.

I.
CARLY RAE BEDLAM

RETROSPECTIVE HOROSCOPE FOR MARCH 2020
(Or, Quarantining at the Banff Centre for the Arts)

Gemini, you can resume eating for two. Your dorm room
is not your womb but sick weeks trip into trimesters.

You will not labour into the hall for seven+ days,
just enough time to create a new world or

as incanted by the magazine *next* to the one you like,
lose seven pounds. You may do *one* of these. Gemini,

you no longer have to worry about the neighbours
hearing you sing along to Carly Rae Bedlam. But

who will you imagine is watching you shower,
hearing you whisper lisped, smelling what you spritz
                                        on those
                                        limp wrists?

            Your ruling planet
            is Uranus.

Around the 20th, you'll run low on prunes
but room service roughage will do.

Therapy asks: *ought* you to suck a virus
into the lifeblood of your death?

Will you fail?
Finally take a D?

A measuring tape will tell you to strap on
boots, you Twinkle Feet, for the 15' x 20' laps

your room permits.
Take a hike.

Or
not.

Your sororal self once dated a pro-life twin, Gemini.
The other twin came queer a few years later,

their other sister too. Brother holds out.
But you think everyone is – no, everyone *can*.

Remember this is a faith mode,
a gift for seeing potential.

Lucky numbers: 44, 36, 413. Must we
trace a tendency to a primal scene?

Monday, you may think so.
Tuesday, Freud you are not.

Gawd love a prohibition. Don't don't
don't tell Mom the babysitter's [   ].

You are still full of that house.
This month might not go swimmingly.

There are not so many
Pisces in today's sadder sea.

Hooked, or is it tied up,
let the mountain air-dry you free.

DORM-ROOM ISOLATION

Instead of fucking you, I have
a shower, which is suddenly easy,
imagining you on the ottoman
across the room watching. Now
the quarantine scrub rubs
me all the right ways.
Queer twins sing for me
to come closer and I will in
four-to-seven days, or in other
cities, realms, cafes, whichever
or whoever comes first. What it took
these years to get me under the nozzle,
when all I needed was a way
for getting clean to be dirty.
Last lesson to slip in the file marked
"Superfluously Belated."

Instead of you fucking me, I study
an encyclopaedia of pasta, dozens
of shapes and names my tongue
can't say but would like to taste.
When I'm cold, I want your radiatori.
Breeze your breath into my orrechiette.
I hear you. I throw ditalini like confetti.
          [Near rhymes + two metres.
          Both are close enough for today.]
Day Two of quarantine,
I memorize seventy-three pastas –
must be ready for second base
and Double Jeopardy.

Instead of us fucking, I dither.
Consider the power
of negatives, the trace
that wasted potential leaves.
You are all sharp textures

pricking your black t-shirts.
To contextualize means "to weave."
I have lost the chafe of social fabric.
Are they empty tanks that drive me?
Today I felt so much of
you not inside me. On day three
of quarantine, I do not yet
escape from this cave.
But I am clean.

OHBIJOU

She slugs herself slowly to
a song she says builds.

Offbeat is fun but tell me what's better than
a steepening snare directly on the trigger.

Creature, I'll catch you
gently around the neck.

I download therefore I transpose myself
into a musicologist of her tempestuous signatures.

Music is a learning aid in the
sexual pedagogy of pandemic. Lesson Only:

> infinite *da capo*;
> admit no *logos*.

A beat coerces. A throb orders us
into uncoiling choreographies of the actual heart.

Cadence is the lead-and-follow game of the gut
we play across our gaping providences.

My embouchure is a rusty rosary.
My lungs once held balloonfuls.

Now arousal inflates like a bouncy castle let go
indoors to fill every corner of my rented room.

She makes no space for sweet melodies.
Already knows she would be becoming when

coming on me. Flouts my mouth
at least once a day. I didn't think

I was dramatic, but I have twice or
once been the silent yes at the end

of a problem play. Save your breath
for fiercer fermata endured indoors.

I am fat enough to float
us both ashore. I have loved

three lifeguards, but still think
I don't want to be saved.

        Yeats:
                Hands, do what you're bid:
                Bring the balloon of the mind
                That bellies and drags in the wind
                Into its narrow shed.

I loop her song around me
and undo my belt. Like most,

I'm not sure what I expect
to find in here, but I look.

EMOTION

The Buzzfeed quiz asks which album
"the gays just won't stop talking about"
and the correct answer is the album
I just won't stop talking about. Oh, to be *seen*
by a screen would seem to mean something
obscene. What could go awry giving me
infinite wifi? My taste in leading men
in teen movies of the '90s predicts how I will die: drowning
in Nutella. I'm tantalized to know it. Another day, an MD
counts how many times my heart throbs in one minute
and tells me what synthetic potions might slow it.
One diagnostic tool is as good as another.

What can one expect to be if Joan Crawford is
the name of one's mother?
Joan Crawford's Kids.
That's a cover band. No, a cover-up.
It's the radiography department's pile of
pink-patterned nipple band-aids (used even for
trans guys whose Jewish ancestry demands
annual mammogram and biopsy). My main squeeze
is a topsy-turvy one; real men are curvaceous
and know all the right ways with long leather laces,
know it's foreplay to trace nascent moon phases
from a dingy on the Kennebacasis.

It's not the size of your capsized ship but your
anti-devotion to ventriloquized emotion
that tells me which capsules to skip.
Whipped creams of what flagellant crops?
If *you're* more BDSM than DSM, drop your props,
throw your hands up. If your wrists are tied down,
you are in a dungeon or a psych ward. Stop. Submit
your best poems by the deadest line listed below.

"Everyone has a British breakfast
that matches their personality. What's yours?"
You say scawn, I say scone, you say Canada,
I say atone. The bacon is streaking again.
I've made a hash of sanity. My eggs remain, if
cracked-hard-boiled. I'm not yolky. All I hear is
my limp's beat, like a trochee. BEDlam. REDrum.
Cowboy mountain's custom phantoms.
Yiddish Christmas lay-off juncture.

Inkhorn darlings taking pleasure
in a world in which half-price parking
for oncology patients is called Generosity.
Fortune is not yet being the brain in the jar.
Joy is permission to sing in the psych ward:
ninety-nine bottles of tears on the wall
(Ninety-nine bottles! Of tears!).
Take one down, pass it around,
and, in the morning,
call me, maybe.

LESSER-KNOWN WELLNESS WORKBOOKS

How To Achieve Nothing & Not Even Post About How Important It Is to Be Unproductive

Take Matters into Your Own Hands: Self-Abuse Is a Better Model Than Self-Care

I'll Stop When I'm Full: How to Fist Yourself Intuitively

The CBT Approach to Not Saying I Love You Too Early or Too Much

The DBT Guide to Fully Justified Skepticism About Gender

Nurture Your Inner Nihilist: An Everyday Guide to Abnegation

The Seven Habits of Highly Annoying People

Un-Unfuck Your Marriage: 75 Charts That Will Help You Realize It Is Over

Strategies For Nurturing Existential Dread

Charts! Charts! Charts! (& Some Info Boxes)

Embrace The Warm White Light

Chicken Soup for Those Who Believe the Soul Is the Prison of The Body

Un-Narrate Your Life (With Bonus Case Studies)

A Step-By-Step Map to Losing Your Reliance on Directionality, With A Litre of Lemonade Spilled on It

Twelve-Week Transformation for Aspiration Addicts: Learn to Live Without the Promise of a Better Future Self

STATEMENT ON POTENTIAL CONTRIBUTIONS TO DIVERSITY

(An Academic Job Application Document)

The Chair of LGBT Studies,
interviewing me for the gig in LGBT Studies,
asked where I identify within the LGBT of LGBT Studies.

I have been L (adjacent), been G, been B, been T, am *me*,
which is not to say anyone's *me* is free of, or beyond,
these dead letters.

I told him I have a finger (usually two) in each pie.
　　　　[four and twenty trans boys baked and too high
　　　　demolish sour cherry tarts with no forks
　　　　before morning goodbyes]

Ergonomic experts agree that
Chairs are bad for the backside.

The next time he interviewed me,
in order to believe, he needed to see.
　　　　You dodged it last time,
　　　　but WHICH ONE ARE YOU?

Coercion: the attribution of irony where
the speaker's joke steps to truth obliquely.

My name is *A Boy Named Sue.*
My identity is *I Don't Know What To Do But I Do.*
My orientation is *Lost and Found in the Lost and Found*
while my gender is a song best sung in a round.
　　　　[sing a song of sixpence / Nana's rye in a pitcher /
　　　　job market kiss of death leaves us / none the richer.]

The '90s saw me squat in Catholic pews
with a secret Jewish history at home, which was

14

the blackberry gash around which one had to pivot.
We had a home and were white. Posthumously,
found an old speech dad wrote for a union convention
in Cuba. Opened with a joke about cigars
and his bad spelling cast no shadows
over how much he let others
(than us) love him.
Did he ever have a job interview?
What do they ask boys with grade ten
before letting them work in the mailroom?
  • Will you die in your 40s?
  • Would you recognize your kids now?
  • Do you exorcise that sore, sore muscle?
      [Two yeses and a maybe, maybe.]

At times, good boys refuse to network, sit in the corner
at the conference reception, eating a mini pork pie
hors d'oeuvres with Saskatoon berry compote.
Some boys get plum gigs but most don't.

I bite my thumb at you who finger
my stigmata faithlessly. O doctor.
Oh dear. My body has long been
public property. I am taxed.
But you can't mortgage me.

At my Edmonton YMCA, folks fled to the front desk to say
they'd spied my penis in the women's locker room.

Seeing is not so easy a business. Believing
is a miracle of weak eyes, wine, organs.

I didn't get the job in LGBT Studies but
I drink no soured grape juice on no altars.

This is all just to say:

Yeah. Students. I cannot prescribe or predict
what may be my "potential for working with diverse
student populations" except to say that I bring my
disintegrating self to work, make only big mistakes,
and allow the same. I show pain. I grieve. I take
late papers. I use written words to show them
that they can experience emotion and survive it.
I know I'm charmed, and cursed. I speak to them
in incantation via poems and comics and films and
novels that are zero degrees from their own knotted ligaments.

My potential contribution to diversity is to offer
the community the benefit of a doubting tomboy.

PANDEMIC LULLABY
~After "Suo Gân," Welsh lullaby~

Sleep, cute girl, amid cutting crisis.
Harm may well come to you,
but I'll be here after, on all your devices
I'll be far away, but not too.

As you sleep, droplets and men spread,
but so does my heart, and yours.
Shutter your eyes, devilish girl;
sleep behind two double-locked doors.

Sleep, sweet crumb, morning is here.
Rest in shallow slumber, at least.
If you can't – well! – we understand why.
Let us anti-heroically slay

> the double-backed beasts that never cease
> to amaze, whose transgressions demand
> enjambment even in songs of soothing.

Be frightened – the leaf that taps, taps,
taps on the door is the harbinger of a fall.
Be frightened; the wave that sighs, sighs,
sighs on the shore is a climate siren call.

Sleep, sleep, though all these can hurt you.
Lay down your vigilance like a heavy sac.
Lay your head on my chest while I sing:
> wakefulness has never stopped the bad thing

Isn't that true?
Know you have company.
The bad things hurt me too.

BOY PROBLEMS

The way they say "pussy" and "tits" as they finger-
fuck you far too fast and uncurious. Wreck me
with beckoning digits curved into my trenches, but
wait for the invitation, and, if not a diction tutorial,
at least a show-and-tell. The way he moves like
he's sure he didn't die yesterday and won't today.
The way he can't grok the belated gifts
girlhood trauma bequeaths. How he thinks
consent is for girls, who need protecting,
how he doesn't know that I might like to
whistle into a blade from that vast field too.
Is there is a worse moment to misgender a guy
than when your hard-on is in his mouth?
Don't file this under To Feel Later. Lay off
the entire department of deferral.
I know what it looks like from the inside.
Have *you* got scars, boy? I've got them too.
Finger those. There, you could suck anything
into DICK, kiss anything GAY. Imagine.

RUN AWAY WITH ME

Gosh, how much running can I do?
I – type 2, type A
to Z, an asthmatic zaftig
too easily left breathless.

This summer's gay soap reboot
draws a distinction between
"running from" and "running to."
Prepositions are the new pronouns.

To and fro is another way to go.
My aerobic videos love the lateral juke –
a football dodge, the mirage that moving
or texting back and forth gets you somewhere.

Let my legs prop up an exhibit on the benefits of lumbering.
I live on kilometre forty of the marathon of the mind.
Tug on my limbs and I will slump apart in steam
like roasted bird. Dry my bones, shake them

in a gay witch's velvet drawstrung bag.
Dump them to read the dirty dice
of gambling me, which spell GO,
GO, GO, GO, GO—YAHTZEE—

PHONE THERAPY #1

The phone therapist asks me which voices in my head
I am trying to not disappoint and I think the answer
is probably—Jann Arden? My wonderdrug traces
my negative phrasings with her tongue.
I'm not known to be insensitive; it hurt
to hear the answers when I asked
if I could be his, or his, girl. No,
it sure wasn't that I didn't
cast any lines towards
that very small pond.

I take notes during this dorm room phone therapy,
on my second-last paper plate, with a purple pen.
Then type seventeen hundred words of notes.
The word-processing software thinks "codependency"
should be "coherency." Relish such a mouthful. Laugh.
Build book castles in your abode
of autoimmune ruin.

Blank cheques are the most valuable. We trust the way
a name narrows WORTH down to the unit of the human body
and its proprietary nurture. An Irish photographer says
      save your breath to cool your porridge
and I wonder if an artists' residency in aspiration would fly.
I sigh to see yet more diagrams of lurid lungs. Inhale
the stale air of my isolation pod after these
seven days in heaven. Make a wish
and blow me over.

I HAVE MY SUSPICIONS

A private investigator telephones
a transgender post-catholic [NOUN]
mid-pandemic. Condo boards sue
landlords sue condo boards,
Former west end renters must bear witness,
distinguish degrees of malevolence.
Was Dante thinking of taxonomy
when he passed from circle to circle?

The P.I.'s second voicemail thrice calls me doctor but
you don't have to ask three times for me to remind you
that most honorifics in the mouth
are worth nothing in a burnt bush.
My crush tells me her cunt is dizzy for me.

Pedagogy: circle lust and gluttony to absolve
yourself of strengthening your obliques.
I do talk to the investigator once.
That's quite enough private dick.

Veronica Mars and Virgin Marys
have done their work: I know
it's me they're after. Finger me
for my crimes. My scholar friend

is on a lifelong quest to locate Jesus's foreskin. I'm no cutter
but I did write a report of my own belated bris. Nancy Drew be-
comes a Hardy Boy. Judas, cast Black in musical flicks, condemns
with a kiss. Clit held aloft on an altar. Do me in memory of this.

Me? Inveterate pop culture cad who insists this is a queer language.
When I changed my name, my friend said it sounded badass,
which she evinced by saying: "Luke Crawford, P.I." My old
Vancouver business cards call me Dr. I never traded them.

Were he alive, my dad might have mocked them.
If he died tomorrow, though, I'd probably find one
tucked in his work cubby at the post office.
It's too on the nose that someone who left love's
expression in limbo laboured at a bureau for
urgent communiqués and dead letters.

Last I saw him, the doctors had ramped down his painkillers
for the afternoon so that he could know we were there. Tubes
protruding, he was hellbent on winking something to me via code.
He felt there was something owed to me. It would be silly of me

to disagree at even this late hour.

I could say that a doctorate in the hermeneutics of suspicion
teaches one how to decipher an urgent eyelid's goodbye. But
my best decoder ring is candied and tells me that the only way out
is to lick things, to investigate the sting of all that unrests unread.

I end every text conversation by wishing you good luck.
With what, you want to know.
I have written bad books about design,
so wary am I of the fever for integrity.

> But I love an argument so let's hear yours.
> A retired Dean of Architecture once pointed out
> that the concept of the THESIS means simply an idea
> that can hold up, stand like a house.

> My legs
> do tire.

> The chiropractor is not sure when
> she can reopen for the season.

> Dad had a big blue ball he sat on
> sometimes – to loosen up.

NOSE JOB

He counted to three and went up my nose with a stick longer
than the smallest of the dildos my Montreal landlord stole.

Great. Now I have a nasal fetish. Dare you
to dig deeper than him and risk reaching

the brain quadrant in charge of [controlling] my
lesser-known appetites. Don't poke a bear's brain

unless you're ready to roar with
cigarettes and chocolate milk.

These are just some
couplets of my cravings.

I'm too used to tracing my own slug trail in imperfect circles.
The elliptical tells me I've grafted well to the world today.

Forty-eight minutes takes you nowhere fast, but
six hundred seconds staring out the window is

a gondola up my own craggy face. In fits of pique,
leave yourself. If you find me dead-hungry on a trail,

bury me in the bones of the fanciest Catalan restaurant.
Ebullition is next to effervescence and my boiling point

suggests I am too far from the sea.
My inner children sparkle at petulant

degrees when the sky is red in morning.
Hard years, I lived just feet from the flood plain.

You can lead a child accustomed to alcoholic ancestry
to water himself at noon with a congregation that speaks

in soft salted tones but you can't make him drink
from your favourite mug shot of you if he's seen

your portrait in the crawlspace.
I can't lie through my nose.

I've blown it again. And
now, I can breathe.

PLEASE DON'T SWAB ME GENTLY

Tug sublingually at the wet quick of a still-sentient me.
Pent up? I'd rather held-down. I'd rather Edmonton

downtown, 2007, dust-dry air in Churchill Square
on a nervous night walk from 97th Ave. I'd rather have

Allie hit my buzzer [*buzzer? I don't even* know *her!*] to
bring me purple flowers. Today, slurping Beaujolais

from her roadways
would be reckless.

Breathless, I await hazmat razzmatazz and all that
my crass bratty boy self can dream in 700 hours.

Day one of dorm room quarantine disturbs
nostalgically. The time I stayed late, alone,

in grade seven, and the teacher let go
a dramatic sigh, to which my freest-I replied,

> I want you to moan like that for *me*
> (silently, yes, but life is the din of its reverb).

Don't swab me gently. Rinse my mouth. Don't use soap.
If it's the last finger I'll taste, you'll dirty it first, I hope.

Test me. I love a high grade,
been feverish to achieve.

Swab me raw, swab rough,
swab slow. Pin me down

with blue ribbons before you go,
so I have something to show for

All.
This.

There is a bowling trophy with a
young girl's name on it, back home.

There is a trove of desperate letters from a '90s crush in
a drawer. I reminded her of a lesser-known Madonna hit.

Sweat comes down like rain when you weigh yourself
against the odds and keep running, westward.

       Banff! You *would* try to be my last home, dissembler
       of habit, firm hand that pulls cotton batting off of me.

       You *would* be my last crush. But there are
       so many of you, and so many of me, and if

       this one, I, sustained a tendency, it was only
       to make myself available to be identified with

            (or against – which remains,
            I do believe, generosity).

II.
FEAST AND FAMINE

I

If Feast ate like Famine, he would get so many compliments.
If Famine ate like Feast, her people would stop worrying. Order
is the disorder of which others approve. Choose your fighter.

SHRUG--   Feast and Famine break bread over broadband,
having ordered the same curry by phone. Famine and Feast
break fast across time zones and from opposite ends of a
medical poster designed by an intern with a thumb up their ass
and the other in humble pie.

SLICE--   Famine likes to split the skin of things,
concentrates her juices to double the recommended daily dose
of Vitamin I. Half a pint of blackberries are dropped in a food tub
outside Feast's door – I cannot tell you what it means – but Famine
cooks dinner and it includes several very adult proteins. Feast slurps
a factory smoothie while Famine milks a walk for a latte.

SUCK--   foodie marrow from a post-plague bone or the
other's extremeness, which is not to say extremities. Famine and
Feast enjoy youth portions of ice cream but in multiple flavours.
They hold each other down and up and will surprise you with even
odder combinations. Feast and Famine work out beefs immediately.
They hate the word but fact is LOVER is a good source of iron.

II

Feast lifts various dumbbells at home: tens and fifteens. Famine
misses her lost pair of 12.5s. This is not an object lesson in balance
or a tutorial in long division, unless you mean "of assets." Are you
interested in developing a new formula for calculating the
square root of Lost? Feast fasts alone in Banff these days.
For him too, hunger feels like being held – but by the wrong person.

Feast and Famine weigh themselves on cattle scales and
kitchen scales, add the numbers together, divide by two,
and finally taste the power of being average. Justice is blind
but she has eyes for weight loss.
"Guilty" is Feast's preferred pronoun,
if it were a pronoun. This will be important
when the drafting of his obituary becomes Writing Prompt #2
in whatever creative writing course tends towards light enrolment.

Famine could stitch a diagnosis into Feast's leather belt
and let *that* hold him in. Feast and Famine have both been
criminally irresponsible. There are only so many interpellations
to which one can turn. Feast's inbox lodges corpulently in
the graveyard of hellish good intentions. His brethren have always
been understood as having stockpiled resources under the skin.

Feast keeps too much on his plate to have the time,
but gobbles last-ditch attempts as at a glory hole in prayer.
Feast has buried the cage of his ribs so that no god could ever
make a man out of him. Famine bears her bones like a canine.
At the grocery, Famine watches a man
buy a kilolitre of chocolate ice cream,
and one of butter pecan. Feast recalls those who prefer
to buy one chocolate bar every day than seven to last a week.
Just a few extra coins to feel that one could be a
better person tomorrow. In this imbalanced age,
one wants, everyday, to be exceptional.

Feast grates Gruyère on
Famine's jagged back.

Fondly, Famine kneads
Feast's front until it's time to rise.

III

Feast and Famine read bourgie cookbooks as satire.
They trade excerpts via text and giggle away at least
seven calories per minute or roughly half as many as
they burn jerking off remotely. Famine doesn't need to
twist Feast's arm or words to get him where she wants him.
Author says that three eggs are practically an orgy.
Feast and Famine will not invite Author to their next party.
Famine wonders about the person who pressed Author's book
urgently into her small hands as a gift. Famine recalls
pornographic novels written with all the eroticism of
a grade ten biology textbook. Feast remembers his high school
of one thousand that had neither cafeteria nor potable water
nor grade ten biology textbooks that did not need to be
shared three ways. Feast and Famine were not yet
Feast and Famine, per se, when they had to step up to the buffet
and pick and peck and point to boy cooks in their twenties
to request their portions. There is nothing intuitive about eating.
But Famine and Feast both sense there is something that only they
know they don't know. Is that what it means to be ready?

IV

Famine and Feast each fast when the craving caves in
but for what goddamn gawds?
St. Francis Caracciolo prayed prostrate before the altar,
incanting in Italian, *the zeal of thy house hath eaten me up*
  [Tabarnak! It's so easy to be digested, architecturally?
  Then let a domicile's bad bones crush me.]
Feast is fastidious with laundry, likes it twice a week,
but lately stigmatizes his pants too often, if organically.

Feast and Famine fascinate, if only each other,
with regular pledges of inconsistency.
Contradiction punctuates their thumbed-out manifestos
of collaborative detachment like thumbtacks lost.
Watch your slow step around fast friends.
Famine fastigates, wants to taper to so many pricks of a finger.
Feast could use Famine's good points to test his blood sugar.
They sip his sweet lipid drink but voice no covenants.

Feast would have liked to be a fast girl
who paid less heed to verb tense. Famine models underwear
and hypervigilance. Feast wonders what protection they will need
when their words flesh out down Davie.
Feast is fat while Famine is fast.
Yes, fat follows fast in lesser dictionaries,
but chronology is an unconvincing caller.
They each suspect they'll talk tomorrow but please
let them believe they can become anything but steadfast.

Who fastened them together like a button
slid through a satin-stitched hole in a too-tight shirt?
Who said fastening would not, also, hurt?

V

Feast and Famine grieve the necessity of insufficient words,
of their geographical distance that grows each day,
drifts into the lower notes of their respective mountain ranges.
Feast once knew a squeezebox player who became deputy mayor
on the strength of a corporate potato chip contest. Imagine him
hunched-drunk and one accordion handle
stretching for the bass note floor.

While shooting cinnamon elixirs,
Feast danced in a Celtic town
to a jam band's fourteen-minute track
about astronauts wanting to fuck.
Famine says she goes to space when the nurse administers
the heavier drug and when boys talk of her as a collectible.
Feast watched hockey as a girl but does not gather rookies.
Firsts are the worst and lasts never last.
Feast stares at his grounded feet.
Famine squints pane-ward.

Beets tilt sweet when roasted but etymologies
twist tongues into the guttural. Famine and Feast
have wanted to end. Have managed not to straighten
or defenestrate. They dig roots.
GRAVITAS means nothing
but grave; gravity; weight.

III.
FURTHER GASTROPOETICS

A BETTER POEM ABOUT PEANUT BUTTER—

Sees it smeared in all our [ACTUAL] scars, not to cover them
but to concentrate tongues and tempers. Spreads it on
deep-fried celery, would stir it into me and my spicy
stew that is just now begging bones to surface.

Hearkens to its use as pinesap remover in the garage.
How I loved for rooms and purposes to collapse on my hands.
Would be written with the elbow grease it takes to scrub
hydrogenated oil from a horde of tablespoon measures.

Excites like first-time Nintendo. Luigi's cock twins mine.
You plumb its depths and I hope won't find I'm just full of shit.
Announces in caps that no princess is in no other castle,
even if we're all locked inside and growing out our hairs.

Remarks that peanuts grow in lowly ground dongles,
neither triumphant tree nor sexy subterranean.
Lets us taste it in gelato on a silent Yaletown bench.
Lists the calories, but in Wingdings.

Preserves the oral history of my schoolyard's rural legend:
the girl who used peanut butter to lure her dog to make her come.
[A myth transferable to anyone except if she had
already been rumoured to fuck frozen frankfurters.]

Uses it to catch overgrown roaches in basements at Western. Shows
me sucking it off my broken finger in condemned Montreal co-ops.

Wraps with Nigella gliding downstairs in silk
to finger a taste "at midnight" for onset cameras.

Deconstructs the natural/artificial binary. Revels in
the organic fact that to undo separation, we stir, and stir.

Defines your every slice as circumcision.
Engages the core and repetition and repetition and

Substitutes kitsch for kitchen, goes jelly-kneed
when you say you need to jam up all gaps.

A better poem about peanut butter doesn't end
with the ragged idea that we HAVE each other.
Includes no domestic scenes.
No glop about staying or leaving.

A better poem than the famous one
that I sent you to flirt – and you hated –
would stick you to my ribs and
I to the roof of your doubt.

WAYS TO SPREAD STRAWBERRIES

Pickle the pale green ones –
guillotine them across
our salad days. We aren't
getting any. During a pandemic,
younger people stir jam crazily;

they squirrel crushes away
then dig up ten percent at most.
Roast my chest over the flame
of her sacrilegious heart.

She thinks I'm waiting for an enchanted word.
My tongue knows many tastes, though,
and history shows sweetness
in excess aches the teeth.

A man who made dentures
just made my province unknowable
but then Nova Scotia always was to many.
Prosthetic teeth are necessary
unless one is satisfied with only
unctuous foods.

UNK-SHOO-US: greasy, oily, servile.
I submit fatly before her
the humble trivium that audio engineers
at the potato chip conglomerate claim
women prefer a crunchier chip.
I have not heard a crinkle from her today.

Mom used to say, wherever I was in the house,
if someone opened a bag of BBQ,
I would hear – I would appear. I'm slow
to respond to invitations but I try to come
when called. Today, I'm feeling off.
My ringer is on.

My freezer is full of jam
that does not need to simmer long.
Spread pectin across
my pecs then let me tell you
what he called them the time he did me
in, in his borough, with slippery diction.

I would rather bake shortcakes for a tall girl
whose silence would whip me
if she wielded it that way.

My villainous reliance on
emotional verbs perturbs,
and not just her. I'm sick
of extracting vanilla;
the balsamic reduction was rushed;
stains never come clean.

A fool is what Britons call stewed berries
and Crème Chantilly. Meringue makes it
a mess. Pluck an overripe strawberry
off the lowly bush and press it across
my mouth so that I can better
decompose myself for you.

The therapist says
things don't become real
to me until I write them down,
but I want to let her affection be – what? –
itself.   What a word.

Others try to convince her she is beautiful.
I don't need magic beans.
I will not climb like ivied reason
into the minds of men.
All I know is convulsing with affection
at a photo of her lavender legs as I smell
the blood of a Jewish-ish boy whose
IUD is down, down, down to dregs.

Drag the wine into blood
if you must fuss with ceremony.
Set your goblet of cabernet next
to the Habitant you microwaved.

Did I not say please?
Experimental restaurants always
want to pair strawberries with peas.
Fruit or veg. Words or flesh.
Which do you want? U-PICK.

Or you don't anymore.
The drop-down diversity survey
does not permit one to self-identify
as a Derridean whore.

That's how my cookie
crumples – that's how
her strawberries spread,
onto a sidewalk, a tarmac, a taxicab.

Then they creep up the deco façade
of the repurposed marble bank on
a hundredth street, in which I sleep,
to sow in me. Know that we
shall not be grim to reap.

FUCKING WITH ECONOMY AND GRACE

"Feast and Famine read bourgie cookbooks as satire"
and sometimes adopt a book's tone for other purposes.

I. How Does One Introduce Oneself?

The modern woman, among which cohort
I place some part of my very own self, cannot help
but agree that good fuckery in our time of climate change
and pandemic requires the utmost consideration
of what it means to fuck affordably, responsibly, and well.

We do not need to fuck like characters on television
or the neighbours we hear through the wall and expect
might be stretching the truth with their dirty decibels
and droning groans. We need to fuck like people
who are learning to fuck. We need to masturbate,
fantasize, and fuck like the people we are –
people who are horny.

Luckily, great fucks rarely begin at points that would
resemble beginnings at all. The best things are made this way:
as a tree planted today won't bear fruit for years, so too
must you have faith that even the worst fuck can be
redeemed with patience, training, and care.

Every fumbled handjob is an
apple orchard in the making.

We are all too happy to let loose ends fray and fall about our hems
like leaves in October. We must pick them up and jump joyously
in their piling. Irredeemable sheets need only to have their
stains excised to become stylish throws. Used condoms,
simply rinsed with a 2:1 solution of vinegar and water,
should be the up-cycled balloon animals of the next generation.
Save your nearly spent tubes of lube, scissor each open,

and consolidate in an unmarked tub – you'll be grateful for this
next time the drugstores are lousy with hoarders.

Ingredients must be permitted to topple over into other categories
like drunken aunts after the celebration of nuptials. If we decide
not to relieve ourselves and rinse after a front-fuck, we must not
drain the eventual leftover litre of unsweetened cranberry juice
into the sewer. With a deft glug of agave and pinch of agar agar,
you have an elegant palate cleanser
for your next online dinner party.

But fucking is best approached from wherever you find yourself
when you are horny, and should extend itself long past this page.
If our orgasm will be everlasting, then our only task is to begin.

II. How Does One Learn to be Tender?

I have watched fucking onscreen, factory-farmed,
and while I cannot complain about its purpose,
I protest its over-representation in the erotic education
of our populace. But it is no worse than the waters
of *scientia sexualis*, into which, like any good girl,
I was dipped. The textbook diagrams do not teach us
how to get what we want, or, more importantly, how to want.

I have also watched fucking face-to-face-to-face,
and sustained eye contact with the person my friend was fucking,
while I was fucking someone else. I have stooped to swab up lube
that slicked the floor of the roiled and rich chaos of
queer Montreal play parties circa 2008.

Good fucking only seems so rare when we view sex like
normal people, eyeing only the climax, and relegating the rest
to words as offensive as "foreplay" and "cuddling."

Time remains a problem
even at the end of it.

Most pleasure in bodies can be found in tough cuts and offal,
such as the brain, heart, or trotters. These are hardworking meats
and must be coaxed into tenderness with time, pace, and intention.
Clitorises and penises are largely idle as compared to arms
that uplift and legs that squat at a fridge to review the crisper
for the potential of salvation. They are easy to roast
and even the most amateur sexual partner cannot help but
arouse some interest from them.

The best parts await those with the patience and ethical orientation
required for whole-animal fuckery. Tenderize a calf in your teeth
to see how far legs can take you. Kiss a jaw until it slacks
into relaxation and lay it softly on a lap. With herbs and potions,
massage for hours the parts twisted up and away. A reward
will greet your mouth at, hopefully, the moment at which
you don't expect it. Rub your legs together and smoke the joints

of her knuckle over the heat. Crack her hands open like lobster claws
thrown back for being too small. Tuck your tongue in for the night.

The most delicious bodies are those
that receive affection and sunlight.

III. How Does One Boil Water?

Tell me I should have done better
from my quarantine dorm room and let me
stick my head out into the rain. Acidic drops
sizzle on my *plancha*. That is how one knows
I'm ready, but there is no recipe for this.

I will eat pumpkin seeds, over-hydrate, lay back
in the front yard, yawn long and wait. Split the giant gourd
of me next month and hose it full. Stuff newspapers
all around and light them. Wrap the lesser-liked
mini chocolate bars in tubed dough and stick-roast them
while waiting for bubbles to burst on my surface.

Wet tongue on inner thigh at a time
when time can't stand for the stillness required
amongst wild viruses. Recite tongue twisters
that don't cohere in order to simulate the oral fatigue
I want her to give (yes, give) me. No, really.

Watch.

IV. How Does One Build a Ship?

If one feels there is something intuitively gay about the navy,
they are both correct and incorrect, insofar as we have all heard
the relevant Village People song, know that dick-sucking sailors
numbered in the infinities, have met those navy boys who would
not throw a rope to save a life, would not rock a ship
to loosen a noose. A better poet I know has maxed out
the realm of naval puns already. Allow me to add:
the [poop] deck is stacked against us.

Did I not mention that this is all occurring inside of a bottle?
It's a butch boat, but yes, boys, you must use tweezers
to thread that tight neck. Past that narrow chute,
a waving world opens for patient hands. You could
use the same tweezers modernist chefs use to plate up,
the ones 'rustic' chefs mock as a code
for fruitiness, that soupçon of faggotry.

My eyebrows thicken, unknit you. Lick this
salty crease that remembers my thought.

To build a ship: suck, lick, slurp, gulp –
to dissolve dozens of popsicles.
Gather the sticks then give glue to children.
Let them show you new ways to leak.
Across the room, a poet licks the plate
of a hungry girl with no sea legs.

Good birthday party activities during a pandemic include
feeding her peanuts and fingers, then crafting a conveyance
that could float tons of nothing from landlock to liquid.
No, not an ark. All worthy cargo is singular.

THIRD-DATE PAINT CHIPS

                             Black

Silver Slit
Banff Blush
Scorched Ex
Domicile Dust
Golden Ghost
Roasted Marshmallow Kiss
Oh This? Yes, It's Something New
Burnt Bridges
Bolt Cutter Grey
No Mother; No Pearls
Chewy Chickpea Hell
Walking on Zero Eggshells
Fifty Shades of Masturbatory Mist
Finally Finally Finally Finally Finally Kissing
Boy's Blood
English Bay Beige
Huge Spoon Silver
My Chest Scar Violet
Salted Pistachio Gelato
Co-Conspirator Custard
A Blonde's Pandemic Roots
99 Red Heavy Balloons
Spread Strawberries
Jagged Little Bones
Plate Licked Clean
Stained Shorts
Crushed Nuts
Exerted Ecru
Et-Tu, Cherry Blossom Memory?
His Enchanted Menses
Perverted Whisper
Ironic Tweed Ash
Inner Space
Jawbreaker
Tourniquet

                             Pink

MOTHER'S DAY 2020

Teenaged girl in want of prod, I puddle-jumped generations
to shop for vintage mommy issues. Young boomers
eat old millennials tastelessly. Yes, it's a mouthful.
When asked, an ancient ex said my junk tastes like steak
I was pleased – charred patches, crosshatched marks of grill,
plaits of fat mouth-melted. Metal. If you're going to eat a person,
let them be rare. But she was a sporadic vegetarian. I'd bet
her clumsy wine-dank mouth still stains plusher carpets. Let me
tell the others: they can be removed with elixirs and grease of elbow.

My crush, though – you say your whole body is a mouth,
that taste buds can unseat steady selves. I want to precum
banana medicine for you. Ooze rosewater syrup on your
star-shaped donuts. Fizz like the Diet Coke I crack too soon
while lecturing teens about Frank O'Hara. Detonate
like the homebrewed root beer under my parents' bed
after my dad decided 1/8th a teaspoon of yeast had to be
a typo and octupled it. I will be salty like the corn chips
I crunched while watching a mean older girl shuffle
to a Beatles megamix in a dark school gym.

I will cool your tongue like the peppermint patty
that melted as mom told me at the Acadian Lines bus station
that dad hadn't made it. You can make me do things.
I will wave my orange hanky and let it drop bedside
like the southern belle the faggot of me is. I'm faint
for your smelling salts. Couch us in whatever tongue
you prefer to speak. The beach crashes from you
and we kiss the pacific from my chest.
If they can milk a coconut, it is possible
to blow me. You told me so on Mother's Day.

On today's *Mad Men* rewatch, Linda Cardellini
plays an uppity Italian Catholic mother, crucifix tucked back
for a fast fuck. In *Home Alone*, a panicked Catherine O'Hara
thrusts home in a cube van with John Candy to get to her boy.

I want to taste like a cheese pizza you have all to yourself. Burn
the roof of your mouth, soothe like aloe. I stayed at a hotel
in California recently with a large framed poster for *The Graduate*.
I got lost in ivy air on my way back from a talk. Ann Bancroft
was okay in that flick but Generation X marks my spot.

YOU ARE HERE. At 7-11, plastics sucking tightly
around factory-made cakes that fluoresce pink on my tongue.
In Nova Scotia, we float dumplings on stewed blueberries,
call it Grunt. In 1954, a Chicago teen's cakey version
won a bake-off with streusel and chutzpah: "Blueberry Boy Bait."
Cool it on the windowsill of your legs and wait for me
if the world keeps ending tomorrow.
I will come soon, bearing merry bags and bags of
every alternative milk we could ever need.

IV.

SEMINAR IN MODERNISM
AND OPERA

I. Overture

My new crush does not sleep,
so I rush to write lullabies
to be sung by women or
boy sopranos. I am neither,
even as a girl was loud and low,
vibrating in alto and
a wrinkled choir skirt.

An inside joke of the opera world:
contraltos are cast only as
> *witches,*
> *bitches,*
> *and britches.*
> > But doesn't that
> > sound good,
> > old love?

I've played these roles, sung
same old songs. If it's been long
since I've stolen a scene from downstage,
let us not blame it on my limited range.
If we'd vocalized more, we would have
had our day, you say. Tell me:
is hearing so easy an art?

Were our overtures too high-strung
for ears that young? My signature key
was smarting sharply for you.
Didn't I? Still could. Won't I?
Won't I? Won't I? Won't I?
Ever notice witches, bitches,
and britches don't die – ?

> And who wants [to be]
> a leading man anyways?

II. *Salome*

I'm no castrato, but!
I'd have cut anything off to
chocolate-dip-rainbow-sprinkle
it for your afternoon repast.

Curtains drop; blood runs
from the corners of my smile; Salome
tongue-kisses a decapitated head
for several minutes. Even my ex
says you and I qualify as tragedy.
But no operas have yet been set
in stations of the light rail transit.

Corona Station/Virus. Feelings kept at Bay.
And the Tim Horton's next to our station
that buzzed me into the men's room
no matter what I asked for and never
furnished a lick of toilet paper
for the wet front of me.

Others have borne the brunt of me
and that may be the kindest gift
I laid at your bare feet, which now
stand you erect and pregnant, and
all I'm expecting of life is—what?

My wide wants, so unwieldy.
I have learned that all I use to shield me
can also smother me. I lay down
my arms and legs in a rented bed,
break fast and slowly for bodies
who somehow somewhere got to know
how to be the donut and not the hole.

III. *Oedipus Rex*

Me, Explaining History: I *loved* you!
You: [redacted redacted redacted]!

> Yesterday's conclusion: *she wanted to kiss me*
> Today's conclusion: *she wanted to slap me*

> And tell me, mother: how could
> I ever choose a favourite?

Leadership retreats ask us to plummet
into the bosom of another. Bottle-feed

yourself the milk of human trust and see
if you know how to latch and let go

simultaneously.
You once wrote,

> "trust is dumb. but, then again, we always fall that way.
> lean that way. topple that way. I need it regardless."

I want to cry. Can you hear my voice breaking?
TIMBRE!   TIMBER!   TIMBRE!

> "I feel really lonely all the time too.
> Because I'll never move mountains."

> "You move me and
> I am mountainous."

IV. *Falstaff*

I grew up in a valley. A pyre.
You are only one life I lost
in the fire of the big-bad-holy-father-
wholly-impossible-no-good-selfhood.

Some losses need to rhyme this way,
being so bereft of reason. Fat
country girl of me never felt in season
in the city or near beautiful types.
Undercooked. Overripe. Now,
do I produce juicy gossip?
Let hard hands squeeze me?

Verdi's *Falstaff* had a working title:
"Pancione," or, "The Big Belly."
A farcical fat knight attempts
to seduce two married women.
Comeuppanced, his happy ending is
that he's not the *only* fool on stage.

Rewrite him a success. Rewrite him
in bed with men and women and
genderqueers and anyone
who could teach him his body
magnetizes as well as any other.
Let him imagine company
that does more than love
misery. Let him. Let him
have done it sooner.

   Yet,
     Tutto nel mondo è burla...
     Tutti gabbati!...
     Ma ride ben chi ride
     La risata final

V. *Madama Butterfly*

Content warning Puccini might have included:
orientalism, racism, sexism, self-harm in the extreme.

She stands on her shores waiting for her white man to return.
Leaves her baby to him and his white bride, tucks an

American flag into Baby's hands,
launches herself swordward.

You in 2007:
> "Babies give me the creeps. Like why why why
> do they have to come out so floppy and why why why
> do they 'nneeeeeeed' women to be women soooo much."

Is it a relief that we change?
That we also recur?

Operas dig martyrs. But I've dug
my way out of that old routine.

So don't expect me to enjoy this pain,
starting any moment now any moment—oh,

I would fly but transgender cocoon
metaphors cause much fatigue—

VI. *Porgy and Bess*

We belt arias in public squares of the heart,
in the heat, in several summertimes.
I never thought your living was easy
(for the broke broke broken record).

["Summertime" – a downbeat lullaby sung by a Black mother
for a Black baby in an all-Black-casted opera by a white composer
for a pretty pale audience in 1935. As with much else, it is not
for me to say what this means but we could remember it.]

I limp arrhythmically but I am not Porgy,
"disabled Black street beggar."
You are not Bess or Clara.
Do you ask your babies not to cry?

Hush, poet. Put on a soundtrack.
A playlist. A memory. And listen.

VII. Recommended Supplementary Listening

Imagine the cacophony if we had
stepped out hand in hand or my hand
in your back pocket or your hand in my
hair or our hands, in any case,
no longer pocketed
by nervous cloth.

Schoenberg's *Second String Quartet*
elicited much [BOO] much [HISS]
because he kissed away
the notion of a home pitch.
No key, no tonic, no woman,
no cry, no supertonic, no super-
ego, no id, no fat maritime kid who
would be honoured even to audition
for second fiddle.

Our letters from back then
had at least a dozen tones.
Lady Gaga has just released
Chromatica. Nightly, I grind
my kneecap down to paste
dancing while it rains outside
on the sidewalk where
we once let ourselves eat cake,
on the shuttered-up dyke bar
where so much nothing gyrated
directly on the sweaty beat.

VIII. *Salome* (Reprise)

My new crush is curious about you.
                    Why express love as a regret? . . .
                    Let it never be that way with us.
I agree.

One ought to have only one operatic love per lifetime.
One with whom love is a pre-existing condition
foretelling death, is a matter of potions, spells, accidents,
betrayals, is a performance of acts, of intermissions,

of intercession. I pray to Saint Salome. Note, students:
she does not wish for St. John the Baptist to be her lover. No.
She can only kiss him once he is dead.
She can only want his head on a silver platter.

You said I was too smart for you, and I knew
already that my brain was my alibi, knew
it had to make good on all the things
for which my body owed apology.

[Oh hey, by the way, I just took a poll
of everyone who knew us then and they
agree you didn't see yourself any better
than I saw me. SO THERE SO THERE SO THERE –]

IX. *Tristan und Isolde*

Wagner's *Tristan und Isolde*
plays the most famous chord
in modern western music.
As you know, "the *Tristan* chord"
resolves dissonance with
a different dissonance with
a different dissonance.

The Tristan theme opens and closes
a Lars von Trier film that foretells
the end of the world. Kirsten Dunst
marches through marshes
with a wedding dress on,
lies down in the river
like a corpse.

The theme plays. Earth explodes. Ouch. Definitive.
No suspension of desire. No denial of resolution.

Well.   Most people would rather the
          planet pop than live in limbo.

               But it is all we have:
               one odd assortment
               of notes to the next and
               the next. Let go, then,
               of the fever for making it new.
               We were never new, and won't be.
               This means, too, that nothing
               ends, that nothing can. All the pennies
               are gone and all the vinyl is scratched.
               So come suicide come plague and
               all my other silly words and things,
               it just ain't over 'til the fat ~~lady~~
               the fat ~~lady~~ the fat ~~lady~~ the fat
               ~~lady~~ the fat ~~lady~~ the

V.
MUSTER POINTS

INSTRUCTIONS FOR IDENTIFYING YOUR LOCATION IF LOST

Reincarnate the first time you let a person
who wouldn't stop touching you (who you

didn't want touching you) stay the night,
because otherwise they're driving home drunk.

This is my body; I give it up for – what? Gerrymander yourself
so that you just can't get the vote. Ownership is a hoax. SAD!

I'm not a democracy. I'm a cheer-o-cracy
on the flat earth of enforced happiness.

What did he call the sticky of me in which he would enforce
Reddit orthodoxy? *I'll rip off her fake dick and rape her straight.*

I am told that line might shock you. I am not
in the business of telling you not to be upset.

O how we retune our ears to bear
polyphonic sidewalks and stalls.

On other coasts, deans point to blue telephones on a map,
advise against worry. My death threats live in everlasting escrow.

Condemn yourself not to the slower death of exhaustion
committees intending neutralization of enemies. Return me

to 2001 and let me major in critical approaches to coupling and toppings
(praxis: two-for-one pizzas on James Street). Regress

further. Dr. Seuss. WWF of the early '90s. Neon.
Rowdy Roddy Piper picked a patch of salt and pepper curls

and put them on me for good luck.
First-fuck, fast-fuck, fist-fuck, friend-fuck.

Alliteration is a literary device the effect of which
cannot always be predicted but may include the

creation of a hard, fast, pounding rhythm.
An unlikely pulse that persists.

Waves. Orbits.
Homing.

"YOU WILL BE TRAVELLING TO DISTANT LANDS FOR BUSINESS PURPOSES"

My bra, if I wore one, would house
the fortunes I pulled from the cookies
while I laid, talking to you, " . . . in bed."

But sweaty beasts dissolve papers of all
legal and otherwise binding magnitude,
let me tell you. So I would laminate them

at the office-supply mega-mart that used to stand
where the arena does now. Then I would meet you
at the dyke bar with the unmarked door in the alley

two blocks North, outside of which cops once pulled over
two lady profs for picking up a graduate student
who had been walking home. My black bra,

when I wore one, shone faux-silky in a drag number
at that bar. My butch comrade and I tore open our tops
in order to bottom for all eyes one or two times.

Once, the show-time chest binding
about which I was most lackadaisical
came undone in an on-stage strip.

I'm warmed that my
worn grey sports bra
got its day in the smoke.

air out your wounds,
the doctors say.
Who has the time?

Mom stares (smiling) at a woman who
stares (smiling) at me over lumberjack slams
at Denny's, drunk, post-show.

The boy at the grocery thought my name was Lucky.
And I do have people who love the people
who love me – just for loving me.

High school, the marching band took a bus to PEI for a week
and I forgot to pack any extra bras. But didn't need them
for fishing with other fat jagged girls using a stick and a string.

One of them told me later that she's queer.
Then she stopped talking to me.
Now she has many children.

I wouldn't have touched her with a ten-foot metaphor.
Didn't want to. Who attends the phantom funerals
for such lost potentiates as these?

Grieve those who err
on the side of the safe
bet. Ante up

and light a candle for unborn queer cumshots.
They are special orgasms.
Let them live.

The house – yes, the house – tends to win.
Even as a ruin. I have lived in the Colosseum
of heterosexuality's dead air.

> Now I travel instead to distant lands
> for business purposes – to see my one

with the feminine bra, which was given to her by a man who
couldn't grok that a feminine bra is not what she would want.
She lives dangerously in the valley of uncanny dissemblance.
Toggles between a man and a greased chute to Mars and me.

Now I clasp my strapless bra of prom night,
ask how it could dare defeat an
attraction as strong as gravity.

The phone therapist says not to change
my wants but to wrap them anew. Most
wear the wrong bra size their entire life.

The best approach to tits seems to be ambivalence
if one is bored by knowable orbits. So many straps
to hold in what we could otherwise become.

They slide further and further down. I am reticent
to ask anyone to pull them back up for me.
Please tell me who I will have been.

      Another cookie tells my new astronaut love:
      "People will find it difficult to resist your propositions."

TIGERLILY PERFUMERY, 973 VALENCIA ST.

Whoever she or I fuck or don't or will
or won't, or wouldn't or couldn't,
the power of cross-category connection
in cities where women feel permitted
to presume faggotry should not
be underestimated.

I nose several hundred nozzles and
she delights in my delight, then tells me
of her dead dog, favourite breeds.
        You seem to like the more culinary-leaning scents—
Her assessment does not startle me but talking tastes
with strangers always slaps synaesthetically.

        Someone floats in, introduces themselves as Cloud.
        I could see almost anything in their shape.

I carry out modern translations of the Body Shop's "Oceania"
and of the discontinued "Vanilla" that made people wonder
who was baking cookies and how. Stark juxtaposition coming →
Two blocks over, a cop's unsheathed gun fixes on a Black man
who had called them for help. This is what I saw. It is not a reference
you are missing, and it did not make the news.
If included in a poem,
this image should certainly be upsetting
in that racism and murder
are upsetting and ought to be.

Pandemics are never distributed equally.
On a mountain, later, I find free samples in my boutique bag.
"A City on Fire": burnt matches, cardamoms, dark berries
dressed in cade oil, spikenard seeped into clearwood.
I'm thrilled to have sexy-milkshake potions while high-risk
heart-brokering and isolated a fortnight in a dorm.
The score remains plain on the scoreboard. My dad
might have planted the grass on the field, but I never will.

"The Soft Lawn": tennis balls, clay, vetiver.
I miss her and do not believe that missing
should exist in direct proportion to
time spent with a person, place,
or thing. Our era is one of exponents.
The battery drains midway through
my first auto-haircut.

"Bull's Blood" shatters
on sick streets and viruses
become us. Like tigers we
commit to stubborn stripes and
like lilies we [cannot]
attend funerals.

MEETING OF THE ANNAPOLIS VALLEY BOYS CLUB

Two dicks among us three assholes
(who our mutual ex loved). Let me be

fair. We're not all assholes, actually. And I say two
dicks instead of three because of me. But not

for the reason you may think. Hagiographies
of myself are not my post-catholic fetish.

> Valley Boys are not interchangeable. One
> of us inhabited his anal realm loftily, squatting

> at the metal rat maze of his gallery's back
> door. Pay what you can is not the crack

> in the system they wanted it to be. One of us
> aspires, if nervously, to utmost penetrability;

> you never know when you'll be left
> in want of things to want.

"Types" are boring, but most do have one,
even if it's a very loose sleeve, EG.

> boys from towns knee-high
> to Halifax, who make art

> and lack at least one of:
> a dick / a head of hair / a heart.

Triage us, this set of negations that
cannot be wiped clean. I cannot reach

through time with bleach to acid-
wash [my] distressed memory.

Other valley boys enrol
or milk the prairie.

Strawmen and friends of Dorothy don't
need twisted arms to flee a field for viability.

Valley boys are no series, no trilogy of which
South Mountain ministers forewarn the youth.

We can rhyme off litanies of apple types,
bake tart pies out of two-timing times.

We abscond – or don't – make
sweeter parties in kinder kitchens.

No asshole has the same wrinkles, but
there are rhythms, hymns of valley boys

who come home – or don't –
with one of a variety of itches.

THE WESTIN

Tithes thin.
This stint hits.

The hets snit with
these new-hewn tests.

She nests with wine,
ties his white tie in tenths.

His nite in: sin with swine,
tines in stew. Tits tint his wits.

She wets his sinew
when he tents. He wins.

He tenses then wets the sheets;
he wins. This sheen is not new. Ew. Eh?

We hint, we whine. When I whet, I
set west these wishes. We shine – in.

GIRLS WHO LIKE ANI DIFRANCO

They tell me to do things with my facial hair and I do them.
They don't tell so much as ask –
>   *why don't you have sideburns anymore?*
>   *what happened to the scruff you had going last term?*
– and I don't do them so much as try.
An early hairdresser called
my hirsute girl-burns my "whiskers"
and maybe I changed salons
the day I changed my name.
The queer coiffeuses in town
offer a "silent" option but
I tend to talk a tempest to
whomsoever fingers my mane.

Girls who like Ani Difranco were at hot concert dates
legally boozing and cruising dykes by the stage
while fourteen-year-old me was trying
to cough up the words *Mom, I'm gay.*
>   Actually, I said *bi,*
>   but in the black and white world
>   of my head these days I wonder
>   when prematurely grey becomes
>   just grey? I feel ever-young
>   despite my bum hip, fat limp.
>   Which is not to be ageist, only to say
>   that when youth is neither easy nor innocent
>   you are perhaps less reticent to see it fade,
>   to let dark roots seep to light.

Girls who like Ani Difranco and I use purple shampoo
because two of us are brassy bitches who aren't girls.
A ~~girl~~ who likes Ani Difranco wants to sweep
my bare body clean with dirty blonde straw.
A girl who likes to make fun of Ani Difranco sang
operatic covers of "Both Hands" to me and I still laugh.
The ~~girl~~ I like so much likes Ani Difranco but not without irony.

~~Girls~~ who like Ani Difranco tell you not to worry
that I'm using the word "~~girls~~" because
that is how they refer to people and
our discourse is our discourse (and
we have plural) even if I hereby
invite you in, Eavesdropper.
Go ahead and gasp,
but in our aerosol era,
we avoid touching the face.

No girl who likes Ani Difranco
is at all the same, save for their
love of Ani Difranco and their
attachments to me.
Maybe that's a *lot*
to have in common.
Though it may be nearly *all*
they have in common.

Some of you were small bodies
shoving stage-ward in Ontario
with sharp tongues in
search of better stories.
You found them,
          then found men,
                    then found me.
I don't know the ideal order
of these supposed treasures.
But when you bury me,
I hope you [don't] all meet,
so that whatever of me that
can be said to still exist
can go, happily.

Which is not to say
you will like each other.
Or that you won't.
(But you won't.)
Only that although you knew

different people through the body I call ME,
I wonder if you will hear my absence –
     I mean, my anguish –
          I mean, my baggage –
               no, my language –
in the low moan
of the dial tone, in
that breathless beat
before all the calls
yet to be made.

THE FOLEY ARTIST

The one hired to replicate our weekend soundscapes
for scenes in our TV show that transcends genres.
Our rom-com-un-tragi-dram-why-yes-
the-primetime-Emmy goes to . . .
Belated Millennial Fat Pervert Prom
                    [Best performance by a duo
                    in extemporaneous fucking]

Yeah, *that* foley artist – the dude who squeezes
squeegees in showers, waves palms at still windmills,
fingers Saskatoon pies on windowsills, who cracks
much Bubly, spills it onto a stale corsage
plucked from 104 Street rubble. He wonders:
                Is this *the sound of*
                absorption? Is this?

He wrings out a quilt while beating on the snare.
        Staccato if you must know. Do not ask why.
        Remember in junior high, how trumpet players would
        press their bells against the bass drum to become an elephant?

Yes, *that* guy – the one who slaps
a fat mannequin's face (hail Penningtons full of grace
and jeggings), who stomps a pint of raspberries
with bare feet on concrete.

Tap dances on airborne LRT tracks.
Tapes a dryer hot-tumbling all my lost tubes of lip chap.
Puts an antique CPAP on a horny rhinoceros.
Flaps a soaked sheet into river valley breeze, lets it freeze.

Smithereens it over Gretzky's statue too.
("It's the most Edmonton thing you can do.")
Feeds a magpie Cheetos? Swears in Yiddish
through a kazoo? Distorts free jazz?

Yes! The foley artist!
I know who you mean!

Oh. Well . . .
he got fired . . .

Because however much attention we pay
to breath, and pay to ears, this
poor sap has paltry sum pink slips because
nothing, including nothing, sounds like this.

ONE DAY, YOUR GRANDMOTHER—

or should I say your Bubbe, your Baba, your Bibi,
or Abuela? Your Lola, your Nonna,
your ancient treasure –
      [but let me tell you, mine had an edge to her:
      stiff upper lipped for a celtic catholic,
      sipping stiff rye and ginger, shushing us during
      the Saturday ceilidh on cable, and from whom
      tied tubes and other sexual selves were concealed]
                         – will tire of a house.

One day, your grandmother, not long for the grass side,
will decide to move. From a Vancouver Special to
a studio in a North Van seniors' building, let's say.
From trophy house of class aspiration to
domestic retirement nest across the bay, okay?
Three blocks from World's most derelict Denny's
and just two from the Italian café where the owner,
who stacks and slathers each submarine, is happy
to leave the peppers off the Classico if you know
to ask. The best people and meats, by the way,
are nutty. Uncured. My saltwater taffy from the
quayside market sticks to my teeth and my ribs
from which could be made so many maritime men.

Your grandmother will keep the strata's furnishings
in the suite. O this sad set for a show not playing
anymore: table perma-set for four and an unused
welcome mat on a floor lustrous with a realtor's
tricep grease. She will keep these things and
you will help her move in and when you leave
you will smooth the duvet because you are too shy
to smooth her hair or to say *I love you* and you will notice,
on the duvet, a copper smudge of crusted blood. Because
while you were busy worrying the realtor was a swindler,
he was on Grindr and this is the very bed on which
a transgender guy welcomed a realtor in through

the front door for the first time in that door's
near-forty years (of rejection by men, of cryptic
polycystic syndromes, of IUDs, IOUs, of
seeking always to renegotiate the lease).

Boy, please: the body
is nobody's real estate.
   You scratch at the blood. Fret.
   You didn't see me coming, you
   keepers of family treehouses?
   Some vestigial gene in me
   wants to sigh *sorry.*
        But I'm not.

PET NAMES

I hear you call your cat a sweet girl and I want you
to call me a sweet girl. This is either the most or least
surprising thing. Tepid epithets are not our love language;
neither is the idea of a love language, or love,
or language – at least any notion that it works.

Sobriquet, another nickname for *nickname*, is French
in origin and means *a tap under the chin*, or, exactly
what you were giving your cat at the time, and ought to
give me, if you would be kind (of mine). Scruff my rough-
necked ways with blood-painted nails and I will lick your
ice cream bowl when I'm finished with you.

Honorifics seem horrific but at least ours neuter.
Nobody would have fixed us up, even though
we are both doctors who despise hospitals despite
the glut of hours we pass there. Men get hard to fix us up
with bandages, masks, and casts – things to *hold in*
when the quick of us is ecstasy. Escape.

I have made snakeskin of so many names.
Been multiple truncations. Of my last name, my first,
of THAT OLD PSEUDONYM. I have been animals of the forest,
of the sea, of all that is sweet in tooth and queer in claw.
I have visited your campsite at night when you forgot
to hang the food in the tree. People fear the dark
but predators bring on the day.

> Who will I be to you? Consider me on call
> for panicked mornings of the mind.

An ER doc once hooked teenaged me up to an EKG
just to prove that I was alive with thread-thin green lines.
(Should we file this under Cardiology or Art History?)
The machine had a factory defect, I presumed. Until

he showed me one odd skip in the beat. Then I knew
the machine was perfect and had read my end, worked a treat.

For the record, I am now
twice that age. Still I throb.
And so do you. And whatever
you call me, I will answer.

REPORT FROM THE INTERIOR

I don't want you in my dreams. I don't want you in my car.
lay back in my arms. let me be your pink pickled beet root.
you made it a compliment when you called me your
ho-phase meet-cute. garlicky charcuterie cures what ails us,
breaks down tough tendencies. (this too is a fibre art.)
we can wait for hard things to yield between our teeth.
lick my bloody lip clean. it's a vibe. it's a mood.
let me suck these crude metaphors. for if i call your lonely
eyetooth a solo artist, it is because i hum its anthem, from
night to noon, from sun-drop to up-moon, thrumming un-
numbly and driven for you, and not 'cuz it's a familiar tune.
o my dear earworm. get out of my dirt. get into my shirt. sway
with me in the burger joint vestibule. kiss me against every
plexi-inflexi wall that's propped up so much that i want, now,
to let fall. get out of my autumn; get into my winter; get into my
sweater; get into my splinter; get into my cells; get into my scars;
get into my near; get into my far; get into my cock. i was born
a door. yeah ok ok, you can knock. linger in me too. let me
be a warped gate you enter through. it's too much imagery!
what's he even mean? sometimes the dishes aren't clean.
and i don't have a spare key. but hey. you. come inside me.

PLEASE CHILDREN, BREAK SOME COASTERS
AND HEARTS

I am careful but I am big. Impactful. I abhor nouns-
cum-adjectives yet I sing them on the stoop of a poem.
The Sound of Music's tutorial in emotion: a virgin's
major scale brings balance to genocides and fathers.

Gretl drops a tomato. Her eyes know to water,
to fear reprimand. I cry seeing it. Familiarity
is a laxative tea that fat-me doesn't drink
with low-sugar jam and the frailest bread.

Children, claim the right to break. Spank the abbey bell
twice for imperfect trilogies. Let your reparative mode be
slow and wary of wholes. We are all cracked up. How else
could the dildo get in? Mother caught a pina colada

lube sample at Halifax Pride, tucked it into a parcel
for me. It is landfilling next to my old dental dams.
There are risks worth taking. But soft! What damage
doth deposit itself lyme-like in my pipes? Don't go hard,

kids—coasters protect, but are, themselves, brittle. Once,
a coaster stuck to my heavy frapp, then dropped, cracked.
Still I sow my wild oat-milked potions. Don't leave a dear mug
on the shelf and forget them if they think "me" *must* be

a name you want to call yourself. Home economists,
how do we plan for the obsolescence of identity?
Let us be in the dominant tone of the mixolydian.
Coax a captain's stern tone by memory. Cursed precocity,

I was fourteen going on flirting-with-thirty-year-olds
for Reasons. But sure: prance in your curtains, urchins.
Just don't climb every anything. Sit on the queer carpet
of Uncle Max's Bachelor Moustache.

Light Baroness Schrader's Cougar Menthol across a rented Berlin bed.
So long. Farewell. *auf Wiedersehen, darlings.*
We're all cast once or twice in a shitty part.
Open with a dropped drink. Ice.

Beginnings are not a very good place to start.

Acknowledgements

Well. My acknowledgements tend to be boring. The juice is in the poems, okay? Nonetheless, I have many enthusiastic thanks to offer.

Thank you to the staff of the Banff Centre for the Arts, where I was serving as poetry mentor precisely when the pandemic became a pandemic. The Centre allowed me to quarantine for weeks, in my room in Lloyd Hall, receiving food drops from the kitchen, as I awaited a Covid test and figured out where to go next and how on earth I could get there. Special thanks to Derek Beaulieu.

Some of the poems in this book were previously published in *CV2*, *The Quarantine Review*, *ARC*, *Plenitude*, and *Best Canadian Poetry 2023*. Thank you so much to the editors and readers of these publications.

Thank you to the entire team at University of Calgary Press, for your great efforts and support. Thank you to Helen Hajnoczky, Alison Cobra, Melina Cusano, Aritha van Herk, and Brian Scrivener. Thank you to the two anonymous peer reviewers, who helped me improve the manuscript. Thank you to Nicole Magas at Zg Stories. Thank you to my friend, the talented Morgan Sea, who created the gorgeous cover for this book.

I will limit myself to thanking the friends, family, and fellow writers I was able to see during the time I was writing and revising. Thank you to: Nathan MacRae, Jane Aiko Komori, Megan Brydon, Carmen Ellison, Lisa Freeman, Adèle Barclay, Alex Leslie, Elee Kraljii Gardiner, KIRBY, Ted Kerr, Harley Morman, Steacy Easton, Toni Luong, Coral Short, Twinkle Backer, Deb Farstad, Allie Karch, Colin Johnson, thom vernon, Alexandra Bailey, Marco Katz Montiel, Michael V. Smith, my new friends at Augustana, Jennifer Crawford, and Joan Crawford.

Enormous gratitude to Derek Warwick for breakfast and to Melisa Brittain for visits.

Thank you to Lauren Tollifson, whose presence in my life animated the late revision period of this book. She has helped me question some of my assumptions about poetry. About other stuff too. Thank you also to Lauren's family.

I met Alyson Hoy the week I began drafting this book. Their company meant everything through the worst and best parts of 2020 and since. Alyson has graciously allowed me to retain their former pronoun in some poems written long ago.

I love you folks. And all of your cats.

Lucas Crawford is the author of an academic monograph and four books of poetry, including the award-winning *Sideshow Concessions* (2015) and *Belated Bris of the Brainsick* (2019). Lucas is Canada Research Chair of Transgender Creativity and Mental Health at the Augustana Faculty of the University of Alberta, where he also leads "Rewriting Ourselves," a project that will provide poetry workshops to psychiatric survivors and inpatients. He is from rural Nova Scotia (Mi'kma'ki).

 **BRAVE & BRILLIANT SERIES**

SERIES EDITOR:

Aritha van Herk, Professor, English, University of Calgary

ISSN 2371-7238 (PRINT) ISSN 2371-7246 (ONLINE)

Brave & Brilliant encompasses fiction, poetry, and everything in between and beyond. Bold and lively, each with its own strong and unique voice, Brave & Brilliant books entertain and engage readers with fresh and energetic approaches to storytelling and verse.

No. 1 · *The Book of Sensations* | Sheri-D Wilson
No. 2 · *Throwing the Diamond Hitch* | Emily Ursuliak
No. 3 · *Fail Safe* | Nikki Sheppy
No. 4 · *Quarry* | Tanis Franco
No. 5 · *Visible Cities* | Kathleen Wall and Veronica Geminder
No. 6 · *The Comedian* | Clem Martini
No. 7 · *The High Line Scavenger Hunt* | Lucas Crawford
No. 8 · *Exhibit* | Paul Zits
No. 9 · *Pugg's Portmanteau* | D. M. Bryan
No. 10 · *Dendrite Balconies* | Sean Braune
No. 11 · *The Red Chesterfield* | Wayne Arthurson
No. 12 · *Air Salt* | Ian Kinney
No. 13 · *Legislating Love* | Play by Natalie Meisner, with Director's Notes by Jason Mehmel, and Essays by Kevin Allen and Tereasa Maillie
No. 14 · *The Manhattan Project* | Ken Hunt
No. 15 · *Long Division* | Gil McElroy
No. 16 · *Disappearing in Reverse* | Allie McFarland
No. 17 · *Phillis* | Alison Clarke
No. 18 · *DR SAD* | David Bateman
No. 19 · *Unlocking* | Amy LeBlanc
No. 20 · *Spectral Living* | Andrea King
No. 21 · *Happy Sands* | Barb Howard
No. 22 · *In Singing, He Composed a Song* | Jeremy Stewart
No. 23 · *I Wish I Could be Peter Falk* | Paul Zits
No. 24 · *A Kid Called Chatter* | Chris Kelly
No. 25 · *the book of smaller* | rob mclennan
No. 26 · *An Orchid Astronomy* | Tasnuva Hayden
No. 27 · *Not the Apocalypse I Was Hoping For* | Leslie Greentree
No. 28 · *Refugia* | Patrick Horner
No. 29 · *Five Stalks of Grain* | Adrian Lysenko, Illustrated by Ivanka Theodosia Galadza
No. 30 · *body works* | dennis cooley
No. 31 · *East Grand Lake* | Tim Ryan
No. 32 · *Muster Points* | Lucas Crawford